Developing

TACTICS FOR LISTENING

Second Edition

Jack C. Richards

OXFORD

UNIVERSITY PRESS

OXFORD
UNIVERSITY PRESS

198 Madison Avenue
New York, NY 10016 USA

Great Clarendon Street
Oxford OX2 6DP England

Oxford New York

Auckland Cape Town Dar es Salaam Hong Kong Karachi
Kuala Lumpur Madrid Melbourne Mexico City Nairobi
New Delhi Shanghai Taipei Toronto

With offices in

Argentina Austria Brazil Chile Czech Republic France Greece
Guatemala Hungary Italy Japan South Korea Poland Portugal
Singapore Switzerland Thailand Turkey Ukraine Vietnam

OXFORD is a trademark of Oxford University Press.

ISBN-13: 978-0-19-438455-1 (Student Book with CD pack)
ISBN-10: 0-19-438455-1

ISBN-13: 978-0-19-438843-6 (Student Book without CD)
ISBN-10: 0-19-438843-3

Editorial Manager: Nancy Leonhardt
Managing Editor: Jeff Krum
Associate Editors: Amy Hawley, Arlette Lurie
Art Director: Lynn Luchetti
Design Project Manager: Maj-Britt Hagsted
Senior Art Editor: Jodi Waxman
Production Manager: Shanta Persaud
Production Coordinator: Eve Wong

Printing (last digit): 10 9 8 7 6 5 4

Printed in Hong Kong.

Acknowledgments

Cover design: Lee Anne Dollison, Maj-Britt Hagsted
Cover photography: Arnold Katz Photography; PhotoDisc;
MPTA Stock/Masterfile; Barbara Haynor/Index Stock

Illustrations and Realia: Doug Archer, Barbara Bastian, Ron Bell,
Chuck Boie, Carlos Castellanos, John Courtney, Jon Keegan, Chris
Pavely, Mike D'Antuono/ Studio Designs, Stan Gorman, Donna Ruff,
Lauren Simeone, Sharif Tarabay, Winson Trang, Gary Undercuffler,
VHL International

Location and studio photography: Curt Fischer, Stephen Ogilvy

The publishers would like to thank the following for their
permission to reproduce photographs:

5/5 Eighty Four, Action-Plus, Bob Abraham/ The Stock
Market, David Ball/The Stock Market, David Barnes/The
Stock Market, Benelux Press/Age Fotostock, Bettmann/Corbis,
Blumebild/H. Armstrong Roberts, Tom Brakefield/Corbis,
Bruce Byers/FPG, Diana Calder/The Stock Market,
Camerique/Robertstock.com, Ron Chapple/Getty Images, Paul
Chauncey/The Stock Market, Murray Close/Movie Still
Archives, Pedro Coll/Age Fotostock, Rob Crandall/The Image
Works, Bob Daemmrich/Tony Stone, E.R.
Degginger/Robertstock.com, John P. Endress/The Stock
Market, Esbin-Anderson/Age Fotostock, Extra Image
Production/ImageState, Robert Finken/Index StockImagery,
Rufus F. Folkks/Corbis, Tony Freeman/PictureQuest,
Geisser/H. Armstrong Roberts, GoodShoot/Superstock, Tom
and Michael Grimm/ International Stock, Richard Gross/The
Stock Market, Guittard/Liaison International, R.
Harris/Robertstock.com, Fritz Hoffmann/ The Image Works,
Hubatka/Mauritus/Robertstock.com, David Hundley/The Stock
Market, Image Farm Inc./Alamy, JFPI Studios, Inc./Corbis, Jon
Arnold Images, R. Kord/Robertstock.com, Stephen
Johnson/Tony Stone, Michael Keller/The Stock Market, Hal
Kern/ International Stock, Barry King/Liaison International,
The Kobal Collection, Bob Krist, R. Krubner/Robertstock.com,
LLC/ImageState, Klaus Lahnstein/GettyImages, Romilly
Lckyer/Getty Images, Llewellyn/Uniphoto, Ted Maheil/The
Stock Market, John-Marshal Mantel/Age Fotostock, Randy
Masser/International Stock, Tannen Maury/The Image Works,
Tom and Deeann McCarthy/The Stock Market,
McCormick/The Stock Market, J. Messerschmidt/H.
Armstrong Roberts, John Michael/The Stock Market, Movie
Still Archives, Paul Mozell/PictureQuest, Orion/International
Stock, Owaki-Kulla/Corbis, Peter Langone Inc./ImageState,
Photick/ Superstock, PhotoDisc, Photofest, J. Pickerell/H.
Armstrong Roberts, PictureQuest, Pictures Colour Library,
John Powell/Alamy, Patrick Ramsey/ImageState, Robert
Harding Picture Library Ltd./Alamy, Michael Rothwell/FPG,
Martin Rugner/Age Fotostock, Rugner/PictureQuest, Tony
Savino/The Image Works, Doug Scott/AgeFotostock, Ariel
Skelly/Corbis, PhotDisc, Jonathan Selig/GettyImages, Chad
Slattery/Tony Stone, Stockbyte, David Stocklein/The Stock
Market, Superstock, Superstock/PictureQuest, Stephen
Swintek/Getty Images, Jeffrey Sylvester/FPG,
ThinkStock/Superstock, Jay Thomas/International Stock, A.
Tovy/H. Armstrong Roberts, Uniphoto, Steve
Vidler/superstock, Bill Wassman/The Stock Market, Jodi
Waxman/OUP, Stuart Westmoland/Corbis, William R.
Wright/H. Armstrong Roberts, Barry Yee/Liaison International

Contents

Scope and Sequence   iv

Introduction   1

Unit 1:   The Weekend   2

Unit 2:   City Transportation   6

Unit 3:   Renting a Car   10

Unit 4:   Parties   14

Unit 5:   Restaurants   18

Unit 6:   Shopping   22

Unit 7:   Air Travel   26

Unit 8:   Health Problems   30

Unit 9:   Work and Jobs   34

Unit 10: Keeping Fit   38

Unit 11: Invitations   42

Unit 12: Small Talk   46

Unit 13: Hobbies and Pastimes   50

Unit 14: Shopping Problems   54

Unit 15: Hotel Services   58

Unit 16: Movies   62

Unit 17: Fears   66

Unit 18: Telephone Messages   70

Unit 19: Touring a City   74

Unit 20: Airports   78

Unit 21: Hotels   82

Unit 22: Traffic   86

Unit 23: Roommates   90

Unit 24: Travel   94

Scope and Sequence

Unit	Themes	Skills
1	The weekend Past events	Listening for details Listening for opinions Listening for key words
2	Transportations Taxis	Listening for locations Listening for numbers Listening for details Listening for acceptances and refusals
3	Car rental	Listening for key words Listening for gist Listening for details
4	Parties Meals	Listening for keywords Listening for gist Listening for details
5	Restaurants Meals	Listening for locations Listening for details Listening for opinions Listening for gist
6	Shopping Department stores	Listening for gist Listening for opinions Listening for decisions Listening for details
7	Air travel Instructions	Listening for gist Listening for details Listening for opinions
8	Illnesses Remedies	Listening for key words Listening for gist Listening for details
9	Work Jobs	Listening for gist Listening for key words Listening for details
10	Fitness Exercise	Listening for details Listening for reasons
11	Invitations	Listening for invitations Listening for details
12	Small talk	Listening for gist Listening for details Listening for sequence

Unit	Themes	Skills
13	Hobbies Pastimes	Listening for gist Listening for details Listening for likes and dislikes
14	Shopping Problems	Listening for key words Listening for details Listening for opinions
15	Hotels Services	Listening for key words Listening for details Listening for opinions
16	Movies	Listening for key words Listening for times Listening for opinions Listening for recommendations
17	Fears	Listening for gist Listening for details Listening for problems
18	Telephone messages	Listening for information Listening for details
19	Sightseeing	Listening for locations Listening for details Listening for opinions Listening for recommendations
20	Airports	Listening for locations Listening for details Listening for opinions
21	Hotel check-in	Listening for details Listening for requests Listening for opinions Listening for complaints
22	Traffic Transportation	Listening for details Listening for key words Listening for solutions Listening for problems
23	Roommates People	Listening for key words Listening for details
24	Travel	Listening for sequence Listening for key words Listening for details

Introduction

Tactics for Listening

Tactics for Listening is a three-level series of listening textbooks for students of English as a second or foreign language. Taken together, the three levels make up a comprehensive course in listening skills in American English.

Developing Tactics for Listening

Developing Tactics for Listening is the second level of the *Tactics for Listening* series. It is intended for pre-intermediate students who have studied English previously but need further practice in understanding everyday conversational language. It contains 24 units. It can be used as the main text for a listening course, as a complementary text in a conversation course, or as the basis for a language laboratory course. Each unit features a topic that relates to the everyday life and experience of adults and young adults. The topics have been chosen for their frequency in conversation and their interest to learners. A wide variety of stimulating and useful activities are included to give students graded practice in listening.

Student Book

In the *Developing Tactics for Listening* Student Book, students practice listening for a variety of purposes and hear examples of different types of spoken English including casual conversations, instructions, directions, requests, descriptions, apologies, and suggestions. Essential listening skills are practiced throughout the text. These skills include listening for key words, details, and gist; listening and making inferences; listening for attitudes; listening to questions and responding; and recognizing and identifying information.

Each unit has five sections. The first section, "Getting Ready," introduces the topic of the unit and presents key vocabulary for the unit listening tasks. The next three sections, each entitled "Let's Listen," are linked to conversations or monologues recorded on cassette or CD. These sections provide task-based, graded listening practice. Finally, there is a follow-up speaking activity, "Over to You," which relates to the theme and listening tasks of the unit.

Audio Program

The complete audio program for *Developing Tactics for Listening* Student Book is available as a set of three Class CDs or Cassettes. In addition, the Student Book contains a Student CD on the inside back cover for home study. The CD includes the listening passages for the final Let's Listen section of each unit.

Teacher's Book

The *Developing Tactics for Listening* Teacher's Book provides extensive lesson plans for each unit, answer keys, optional activities, vocabulary lists, and a photocopiable tapescript of the recorded material. The Teacher's Book also includes photocopiable midterm and final tests, as well as worksheets (one per unit) that offer additional speaking activities. The audio program for the midterm and final tests is included on a CD on the inside back cover.

Test Booklet

The *Developing Tactics for Listening* Test Booklet contains photocopiable tests for each unit of the Student Book. The audio program for the unit tests is included on a CD on the inside back cover.

UNIT 1 The Weekend

1. Getting Ready

What did you do last weekend? Check (✓) your answers and compare them with a partner.

- ☐ went to a movie
- ☐ met a friend
- ☐ went on a date
- ☐ went to the gym
- ☐ watched TV
- ☐ went to a disco
- ☐ played a sport
- ☐ rented a video
- ☐ played computer games

2. Let's Listen 🔊

What did these people do last weekend? Listen and circle the correct answer.

1. He _____ .
   a. went dancing
   b. watched TV

2. He _____ .
   a. met a girl
   b. went to his brother's house

3. She _____ .
   a. went to the gym
   b. entered a bodybuilding competition

4. He _____ .
   a. played with his nephews
   b. went out with a friend

5. She _____ .
   a. went to a party
   b. went to a movie

6. She _____ .
   a. rented a video
   b. watched baseball on TV

3. Let's Listen

Task 1

Did these people enjoy their weekend? Listen and check (✓) the correct answer.

	Yes	No
1.	☐	☑
2.	☐	☐
3.	☐	☐
4.	☐	☐
5.	☐	☐
6.	☐	☐

Task 2

Listen again. What did each person do on the weekend? Circle the correct answer.

1. He _____ .
   a. watched an adventure movie on TV
   b. played video games
   c. went to a movie

2. He _____ .
   a. stayed at home
   b. went to the beach for the weekend
   c. went to the mountains

3. He _____ .
   a. read lots of interesting magazines
   b. used the computer
   c. read an interesting book

4. She _____ .
   a. played in a band
   b. went to a concert
   c. played tennis

5. She _____ .
   a. stayed home and watched TV
   b. studied for an exam
   c. went out with friends

6. She _____ .
   a. visited friends
   b. went to the countryside
   c. went out with friends

4. Let's Listen

Task 1

People are talking about their weekends. How was each person's weekend?
Listen and circle the correct answer.

1. **a.** so-so
   b. terrible
   c. great

2. **a.** disappointing
   b. pleasant
   c. boring

3. **a.** tiring
   b. terrific
   c. wonderful

4. **a.** awful
   b. quiet
   c. enjoyable

Task 2

Listen again. Are these statements true or false? Check (✓) the correct answer.

	True	False
1. a. She won a contest in a music store.	☐	☐
b. She won a trip to Las Vegas.	☐	☐
2. a. They went to a restaurant for dinner.	☐	☐
b. His friend has a very interesting job.	☐	☐
3. a. The park is very far from town.	☐	☐
b. They didn't see any wild birds or butterflies on the trip.	☐	☐
4. a. There were a lot of interesting people at the party.	☐	☐
b. The party ended early.	☐	☐

Over to You: How was your weekend?

Task 1

Work in pairs. Practice the conversations below.

A: How was your weekend?

B: It was great!

A: What did you do?

B: I saw a really good movie.

A: How was your weekend?

B: It was terrible!

A: Why? What happened?

B: My computer crashed.

A: How was your weekend?

B: It was really great!

A: What did you do?

B: I went to the beach.

A: How was your weekend?

B: It was awful!

A: Why? What happened?

B: I had to study for an exam.

Task 2

Ask your partner about last weekend. Have conversations like the ones above.

UNIT 2 City Transportation

1. Getting Ready

Check (✓) your own answers to the questions below. Compare answers with a partner.

How often do you use taxis?

☐ every day

☐ about once or twice a week

☐ not very often

☐ other: _____

When do you usually use taxis?

☐ when I am in a hurry

☐ when there isn't any other way to get somewhere

☐ when it is raining

☐ other: _____

How is the taxi service in your city?

☐ excellent   ☐ very good   ☐ okay   ☐ poor

2. Let's Listen 💿

People are talking about transportation. Listen and number the pictures.

A.

B. /

C.

D.

E.

F.

3. Let's Listen

Task 1

Four hotel guests are calling for a taxi. Are these statements true or false?
Listen and check (✓) the correct answer.

	True	False
1. The caller's flight leaves in four hours.	☐	☐
2. The caller wants to go to another hotel.	☐	☐
3. The caller needs to catch a train.	☐	☐
4. The caller's friend is going to have a baby soon.	☐	☐

Task 2

Listen again. How much will each ride cost? Circle the correct answer.

1. **a.** $14   2. **a.** $12   3. **a.** $15   4. **a.** $18
   b. $40   **b.** $20   **b.** $50   **b.** $80

4. Let's Listen

Visitors are talking about taxis. Listen and check (✓) their opinions about taxi service.

	Good	Okay	Not good
1.	☐	☐	☐
2.	☐	☐	☐
3.	☐	☐	☐
4.	☐	☐	☐

Task 2

Listen again. Circle the correct answer.

1. The thing she hates the most is that the _____ .
   a. taxis aren't air-conditioned
   b. drivers drive too fast
   c. drivers are rude

2. The thing he likes the most is _____ .
   a. the prices
   b. that the taxis are clean
   c. the drivers

3. The thing he hates the most is that the _____ .
   a. taxis are too expensive
   b. drivers don't speak English very well
   c. taxis are not very safe

4. The thing she likes the most is that the _____ .
   a. taxis are comfortable
   b. drivers speak English well
   c. taxis are very cheap

Over to You: How often do you take the bus?

Task 1

How often do you take public transportation? How much do you spend?
Complete this chart. Then compare answers with a partner.

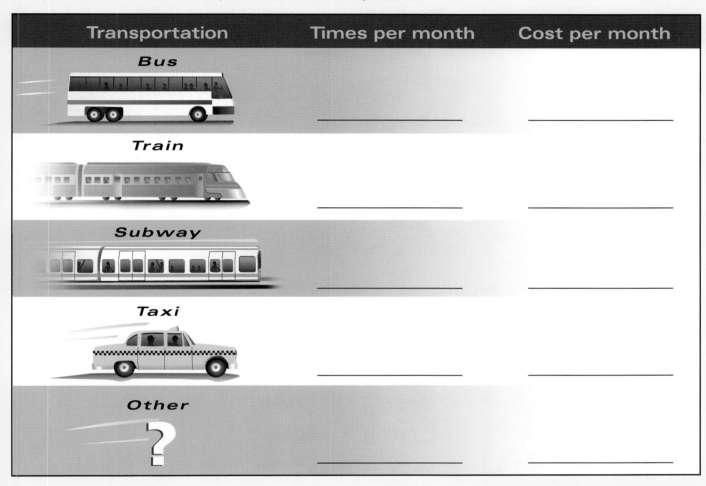

Transportation	Times per month	Cost per month
Bus		
Train		
Subway		
Taxi		
Other ?		

Example: **A:** How often do you take the bus?

B: Every day./Once a month./Hardly ever.

A: How much does it cost you?

B: Oh, about…

Task 2

Ask your partner the following questions.

1. What's the easiest way to get around (your city)?
2. What's the most comfortable way?
3. Which type of transportation do you avoid using? Why?

UNIT 3 Renting a Car

1. Getting Ready

Write the letters of the vehicles next to the correct names. Compare answers with a partner.

1. stretch limo _D_
2. minivan ___
3. sports car ___
4. recreational vehicle (RV) ___
5. station wagon ___
6. pickup truck ___

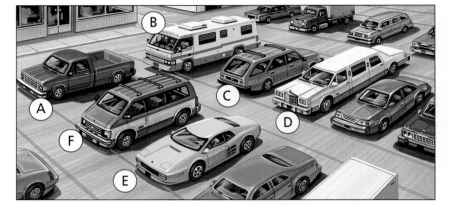

2. Let's Listen

People are talking about vehicles. Listen and number the pictures.

A.

B.

C.

D.

E.

F.

3. Let's Listen

People are discussing cars at a rental agency. Listen and check (✓) the correct information.

1.

Rental period	Size	Location
☐ weekend	☐ small	☐ city
☐ one week	☐ medium	☐ airport
☐ more than a week	☐ large	

2.

Rental period	Size	Location
☐ weekend	☐ small	☐ city
☐ one week	☐ medium	☐ airport
☐ more than a week	☐ large	

3.

Rental period	Size	Location
☐ weekend	☐ small	☐ city
☐ one week	☐ medium	☐ airport
☐ more than a week	☐ large	

4.

Rental period	Size	Location
☐ weekend	☐ small	☐ city
☐ one week	☐ medium	☐ airport
☐ more than a week	☐ large	

Task 2

Listen again. Why does each person want to rent a car? Circle the correct answer.

1. a. business
   b. pleasure
   c. business and pleasure

2. a. business
   b. pleasure
   c. business and pleasure

3. a. business
   b. pleasure
   c. business and pleasure

4. a. business
   b. pleasure
   c. business and pleasure

4. Let's Listen

Task 1

A car rental agent is suggesting different options to customers. Do the customers accept or refuse the options? Listen and check (✓) the correct answer.

	Accept	Refuse
1.	✓	☐
2.	☐	☐
3.	☐	☐
4.	☐	☐
5.	☐	☐
6.	☐	☐

Task 2

Listen again. Are these statements true or false? Check (✓) the correct answer.

		True	False
1.	A large car costs an extra $5 a day.	☐	☐
2.	A city guide costs $50.	☐	☐
3.	The customer is leaving on Saturday.	☐	☐
4.	The customer thinks that the cost of the accident insurance is reasonable.	☐	☐
5.	The customer is the only person that will be driving the car.	☐	☐
6.	The customer rarely rents a car.	☐	☐

Over to You: I'd like to rent a car.

Task 1

Work in pairs. Student A wants to rent a small car. Student B is a car rental agent. Practice the conversation below.

A: Hi. I'd like to rent a car for (1) <u>a week</u>.

B: Sure. What kind of car do you want?

A: Something (2) <u>small</u>, I guess. What kinds of cars do you have?

B: Well, we have (3) <u>a sports car</u>.

A: I see. Hmm...I'll take it.

B: Would you like insurance with it?

A: Yes, please./No, thank you.

B: Okay. Here are the keys.

A: Thanks.

B: You're welcome.

Task 2

Work in pairs. Have two more conversations like the one in Task 1. Use this information.

(1) two days	the weekend
(2) medium-size	large
(3) a station wagon	a minivan

Task 3

Work in pairs. Take turns role-playing the situation in Task 1. Use your own information.

UNIT 4 Parties

1. Getting Ready

**Match each meal or party on the left with the correct description on the right.
Compare answers with a partner.**

1. potluck dinner *b*
2. birthday party ___
3. buffet ___
4. surprise party ___
5. barbecue ___
6. snack ___

a. A small, quick meal or something eaten between meals.
b. A meal in which each guest brings a dish.
c. Food is cooked outside on a grill.
d. A party where a person is given gifts and a cake with candles on it.
e. A meal in which all the food is prepared by the host or hostess.
f. A party which the guest of honor knows nothing about.

2. Let's Listen

**People are discussing parties. What kind of event are they talking about?
Listen and circle the correct answer.**

1. a. dinner party
   b. surprise party

2. a. potluck dinner
   b. barbecue

3. a. surprise party
   b. birthday party

4. a. buffet
   b. birthday party

5. a. buffet
   b. barbecue

6. a. potluck dinner
   b. buffet

3. Let's Listen 💿

Task 1

People are talking at a party. Listen and number the pictures.

A.

B.

C.

D.

E.

F.

Task 2

Listen again. Circle the correct answer.

1. **a.** The cake is homemade.
   b. The cake came from a store.
   c. A friend brought the cake.

2. **a.** She'll play now.
   b. She might play later.
   c. She doesn't play.

3. **a.** The punch does not contain fruit juice.
   b. The punch only contains fruit juice.
   c. The punch contains fruit juice and something else.

4. **a.** He has met the parents before.
   b. He hasn't met the parents before.
   c. He doesn't want to meet the parents.

5. **a.** She bought it.
   b. It was a present.
   c. She painted it herself.

6. **a.** The cat isn't very friendly.
   b. The cat is very friendly.
   c. The cat is tired.

4. Let's Listen

Task 1

People are talking about parties. What did they do at each party? Listen and circle the correct answer.

1. She _____ .
   a. played party games
   b. danced
   c. sang songs

2. He _____ .
   a. watched a home video
   b. danced
   c. ate lots of food

3. She _____ .
   a. danced
   b. sang songs
   c. met old friends

4. He _____ .
   a. played games
   b. ate junk food
   c. listened to music

Task 2

Listen again. What phrase completes each statement? Write the correct letter.

1. The best thing was ___
2. The worst thing was ___
3. The best thing was ___
4. The worst thing was ___

a. she learned some Spanish songs.
b. there wasn't enough food.
c. no one brought music.
d. the music.

Over to You: Planning a party

Task 1

You are planning a party. Decide on all the details. Complete the invitation.

Your Party

Type of party? _____

When? _____

How many people? _____

Where? _____

Music? _____

Food? _____

Activities? _____

Task 2

Work in pairs. Tell your partner about a party you remember.

UNIT 5 Restaurants

1. Getting Ready

What are your favorite kinds of restaurants? Check (✓) your answers and compare them with a partner.

☐ Thai   ☐ French   ☐ Mexican   ☐ fast food

☐ Japanese   ☐ Chinese   ☐ Korean   ☐ other: _____

2. Let's Listen

Where do the people decide to eat? Listen and circle the correct answer.

1. **a.** Chinese restaurant
   b. Fast Fried Chicken

2. **a.** Quick Burger
   b. Pizza Pit

3. **a.** home
   b. out

4. **a.** steak house
   b. Korean restaurant

5. **a.** seafood restaurant
   b. pizza restaurant

6. **a.** Mexican restaurant
   b. Japanese restaurant

7. **a.** fast-food restaurant
   b. French restaurant

8. **a.** home
   b. vegetarian restaurant

3. Let's Listen 💿

People are ordering food in a restaurant. What does each person order? Listen and check (✓) the correct picture.

1.
a.
b. ✓

2.
a.
b.

3.
a.
b.

4.
a.
b.

5.
a.
b.

6.
a.
b.

Task 2

Listen again. Are these statements true or false? Check (✓) the correct answer.

	True	False
1. The customer is not very hungry	☐	☐
2. The customer loves fries.	☐	☐
3. The customer hates spicy food.	☐	☐
4. The customer can't have salt on the fries.	☐	☐
5. The customer wants cold pie.	☐	☐
6. The customer wants lots of sugar in the milk shake.	☐	☐

4. Let's Listen

Task 1

People are talking about restaurants they ate at recently. Listen and check (✓) their opinions about each restaurant.

1.

	Good	Not good
the location	☐	☐
the interior	☐	☐
the menu	☐	☐
the food	☐	☐
the prices	☐	☐

3.

	Good	Not good
the location	☐	☐
the interior	☐	☐
the menu	☐	☐
the food	☐	☐
the prices	☐	☐

2.

	Good	Not good
the location	☐	☐
the interior	☐	☐
the menu	☐	☐
the food	☐	☐
the prices	☐	☐

4.

	Good	Not good
the location	☐	☐
the interior	☐	☐
the menu	☐	☐
the food	☐	☐
the prices	☐	☐

Task 2

Listen again. Did each person leave a good tip? Check (✓) the correct answer.

1. ☐ yes   **2.** ☐ yes   **3.** ☐ yes   **4.** ☐ yes
    ☐ no   ☐ no   ☐ no   ☐ no

Over to You: Eating out

Task 1

Work in pairs. Fill in the chart about you. Then ask a partner the questions
and complete the chart about your partner.

	You	Your partner
1. How many times a week do you eat out?		
2. What kind of food do you like?		
3. How often do you eat at fast-food restaurants?		
4. What's your favorite fast-food restaurant?		
5. What's your favorite fast-food meal?		
6. What other restaurants do you like?		
7. What do you usually order when you go there?		
8. What's the most unusual food you've ever had at a restaurant?		

Task 2

Work in pairs. Imagine that you just opened a new restaurant. Answer the questions
below. Then take turns asking each other about your restaurants.

1. What kind of restaurant is it? _____

2. Where is it located? _____

3. What special food is on the menu? _____

4. What is the average price for a meal? _____

5. How many people work for you? _____

UNIT 6 Shopping

1. Getting Ready

How important are these things to you when you shop? Check (✓) your answers
and compare them with a partner.

	Very important	Somewhat important	Not important
variety of products	☐	☐	☐
quality of products	☐	☐	☐
prices	☐	☐	☐
reputation of the store	☐	☐	☐
service	☐	☐	☐
location	☐	☐	☐

2. Let's Listen

Where are the people? Listen and number the pictures.

A.

B.

C.

D.

E.

F.

3. Let's Listen 💿

People are discussing items in a store. Listen and check (✓) their opinions about each item.

1. Jacket

	Good	Okay	Not good
the style	☐	☐	☐
the color	☐	☐	☐
the size	☐	☐	☐

2. Lamp

	Good	Okay	Not good
the price	☐	☐	☐
the color	☐	☐	☐
the size	☐	☐	☐

3. Watch

	Good	Okay	Not good
the style	☐	☐	☐
the color	☐	☐	☐
the price	☐	☐	☐

4. Sofa

	Good	Okay	Not good
the size	☐	☐	☐
the color	☐	☐	☐
the price	☐	☐	☐

Task 2

Listen again. Do the people buy the items? Check (✓) the correct answer.

1. ☐ yes   2. ☐ yes   3. ☐ yes   4. ☐ yes
    ☐ no   ☐ no   ☐ no   ☐ no

4. Let's Listen

Task 1

A salesclerk is describing things in a store. Listen and circle the correct information about each item.

1. The microwave oven _____ .
   a. has a 3-year guarantee
   b. is sold in many stores
   c. is made in the United States

2. The jacket _____ .
   a. is washable
   b. is made of leather
   c. comes in two different colors

3. The TV _____ .
   a. is made in South Korea
   b. is cheaper than a regular TV
   c. comes in two sizes

4. The watch _____ .
   a. is made of metal
   b. is popular with business people
   c. has changeable bands

Task 2

Listen again. What phrase completes each statement? Write the correct letter.

1. The microwave oven ___
2. The jacket ___
3. The TV ___
4. The watch ___

a. is reversible.
b. displays popular recipes.
c. can be used for e-mail.
d. can hang on the wall.

Over to You: Shopping questions

Task 1

Work in pairs. Match each question with the correct answer. Take turns asking and answering the questions with a partner.

Questions

1. Can you help me over here, please? _c_

2. Do you sell computer games here? ____

3. Can I pay by credit card? ____

4. Can I try these on? ____

5. Is there a restaurant in the mall? ____

Answers

a. Sure. The dressing rooms are over there.

b. Yes, there's a coffee shop on the third floor.

c. Yes, I'll be with you in a minute.

d. Yes, you'll find them in the electronics department on the second level.

e. No, we only take cash.

Task 2

Write three more questions to ask a salesperson.

1. _____

2. _____

3. _____

Task 3

Ask your partner the questions you wrote in Task 2.

UNIT 7 Air Travel

1. Getting Ready

Work in pairs. Match each item in the picture with the correct word. Compare answers with a partner

1. "No Smoking" sign _H_

2. customs form ___

3. headphones ___

4. seat belt ___

5. aisle seat ___

6. window seat ___

7. safety instruction card ___

8. overhead compartment ___

2. Let's Listen

A flight attendant is giving instructions. Listen and number the pictures.

A.

B.

C.

D.

E.

F.

3. Let's Listen 💿

Task 1

Passengers are discussing a problem with a flight attendant. Listen and circle the correct answer.

1. **a.** There's no sound coming through the headphones.
   b. The sound from the headphones isn't clear.
   c. The passenger didn't get headphones.

2. **a.** There's nothing in the seat pocket.
   b. There's no safety instruction card in the seat pocket.
   c. There isn't a magazine in the seat pocket.

3. **a.** The seat is uncomfortable.
   b. The seat is too close to the TV screen.
   c. The seat is too far away from the TV screen.

4. **a.** Two passengers have the same seat number.
   b. The passenger should be in a different seat.
   c. The passenger wants to move to a window seat.

Task 2

Listen again. Will the flight attendant help each passenger now or later?
Check (✓) the correct answer.

1. ☐ now   2. ☐ now   3. ☐ now   4. ☐ now
   ☐ later   ☐ later   ☐ later   ☐ later

4. Let's Listen 📀

Task 1

People are talking about flights. Listen and check (✓) their opinions about each flight.

	Good	Okay	Not good
1. the airport	☐	☐	☑
the flight	☐	☐	☐
the food	☐	☐	☐
the service	☐	☐	☐
2. the airport	☐	☐	☐
the flight	☐	☐	☐
the food	☐	☐	☐
the service	☐	☐	☐
3. the airport	☐	☐	☐
the flight	☐	☐	☐
the food	☐	☐	☐
the service	☐	☐	☐
4. the airport	☐	☐	☐
the flight	☐	☐	☐
the food	☐	☐	☐
the service	☐	☐	☐

Task 2

Listen again. What phrase completes each statement? Write the correct letter.

1. Next time, she won't ___
2. Next time, he'll ___
3. Next time, she'll ___
4. Next time, he won't ___

a. try a different airline.
b. fly if the weather looks bad.
c. get a seat near the front of the plane.
d. travel during spring break.

Over to You: Asking for things on an airplane

Task 1

What can you ask for on an airplane? Write five more things.

1. _a newspaper_
2. _____
3. _____
4. _____
5. _____
6. _____

Task 2

Work in pairs. Student A is a passenger on a plane. Student B is a flight attendant. Practice the conversation below.

A: (1) <u>Could I have</u> (2) <u>a newspaper</u>?

B: (3) <u>Just a moment.</u> (4) <u>I'll get you one.</u> Would you like (5) *The New York Times*?

A: (6) <u>Yes, please.</u>

Task 3

Work in pairs. Have two more conversations like the one in Task 2. Use this information.

(1)	Do you have	Could you bring me
(2)	a cup of coffee	a blanket
(3)	Sure.	Certainly.
(4)	Let me get you one.	I'll bring you one.
(5)	cream and sugar	a pillow, too
(6)	No, thank you.	That would be fine. Thanks.

Task 4

Work in pairs. Take turns role-playing the situation in Task 2. Use your own information.

UNIT 8 Health Problems

1. Getting Ready

Match each problem on the left with the best treatment on the right.
Compare answers with a partner.

Problem

1. a cold _h_
2. a sore throat ___
3. a headache ___
4. a toothache ___
5. the flu ___
6. an upset stomach ___
7. a backache ___
8. an ear infection ___

Treatment

a. take aspirin
b. gargle with warm water
c. go to the dentist
d. stay in bed
e. use ear drops
f. see a chiropractor
g. take an antacid
h. take vitamin C or cold medicine

2. Let's Listen

People are describing how they feel. Listen and circle the problem.

1. a. an upset stomach
   b. the flu

2. a. a sore throat
   b. a headache

3. a. a toothache
   b. a cold

4. a. a backache
   b. a headache

5. a. an upset stomach
   b. a sore throat

6. a. a cold
   b. a backache

3. Let's Listen 💿

People are asking friends what they take for a cold. Listen and number the pictures.

A. ☐

B. ☐

C. ☐

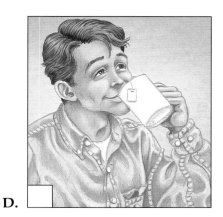

D. ☐

E. ☐

F. ☐

Task 2

Listen again. Where did each person learn the cold remedy? Circle the correct answer.

1. **a.** his grandmother
   b. his mother
   c. his grandparents

2. **a.** a radio commercial
   b. a TV commercial
   c. a TV show

3. **a.** the newspaper
   b. her mother
   c. her doctor

4. **a.** a co-worker
   b. a roommate
   c. a Korean woman

5. **a.** in an e-mail
   b. on the TV
   c. on the Internet

6. **a.** a pianist
   b. an opera singer
   c. a stranger

4. Let's Listen

Task 1

Four people are talking about health problems. Listen and check (✓) the correct information.

1. Patrick

What is the problem?	☐ a headache	☐ a stomachache
When did the problem start?	☐ this morning	☐ last night
Has he had this problem before?	☐ yes	☐ no
Has he taken anything for it?	☐ yes	☐ no
Has he seen a doctor for it?	☐ yes	☐ no

2. Jenna

What is the problem?	☐ a sore arm	☐ a sore hand
When did the problem start?	☐ on Saturday	☐ on Sunday
Has she had this problem before?	☐ yes	☐ no
Has she taken anything for it?	☐ yes	☐ no
Has she seen a doctor for it?	☐ yes	☐ no

3. Kenneth

What is the problem?	☐ an eye infection	☐ an ear infection
When did the problem start?	☐ last week	☐ last weekend
Has he had this problem before?	☐ yes	☐ no
Has he taken anything for it?	☐ yes	☐ no
Has he seen a doctor for it?	☐ yes	☐ no

4. Alexis

What is the problem?	☐ food poisoning	☐ a stomachache
When did the problem start?	☐ two days ago	☐ two weeks ago
Has she had this problem before?	☐ yes	☐ no
Has she taken anything for it?	☐ yes	☐ no
Has she seen a doctor for it?	☐ yes	☐ no

Task 2

Listen again. What phrase completes each statement? Write the correct letter.

1. If he's not better, he can't go to ___
2. If she's not better, she won't be able to ___
3. He has to ___
4. She probably won't go to ___

a. play tennis.
b. play in a band.
c. his friend's concert.
d. her friend's party.

Over to You: How are you today?

Task 1

What are some health problems people may have? Write five more problems.

1. _a headache_   3. _____   5. _____

2. _____   4. _____   6. _____

  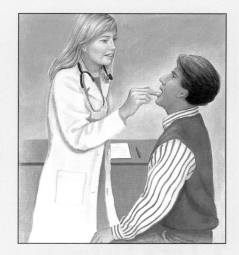

Task 2

Work in pairs. Student A is a sympathetic teacher. Student B is a sick student.
Practice the conversation below.

A: How are you today?

B: Not too good. I'm afraid I can't come to class today. I have (1) <u>a headache</u>.

A: Oh, I'm sorry to hear that. Why don't you (2) <u>take some aspirin?</u>

Task 3

Work in pairs. Have three more conversations like the one in Task 2.
Use this information.

(1) a cold   an earache   a toothache
(2) stay in bed   go to the doctor   see the dentist

Task 4

Work in pairs. Take turns role-playing the situation in Task 2. Use your own information.

UNIT 9 Work and Jobs

1. Getting Ready

What will you think about when you look for a job? Check (✓) your answers and compare them with a partner.

	Very important	Important	Not important
salary	☐	☐	☐
working hours	☐	☐	☐
vacations	☐	☐	☐
commuting time	☐	☐	☐
interesting work	☐	☐	☐
colleagues	☐	☐	☐
job security	☐	☐	☐
other: _____	☐	☐	☐

2. Let's Listen

People are talking about their jobs. Listen and number the pictures.

A. ☐

B. ☐

C. ☐

D. ☐

E. ☐

F. ☐

3. Let's Listen 💿

Task 1

People are talking about their jobs. What does each person do? Listen and circle the correct answer.

1. **a.** musician
   b. manager

2. **a.** manager
   b. bellhop

3. **a.** TV producer
   b. chauffeur

4. **a.** technician
   b. secretary

5. **a.** reporter
   b. photographer

6. **a.** cashier
   b. waitress

Task 2

Listen again. Circle the correct answer.

1. He _____ .
   a. does not have a lot of experience
   b. has been working there awhile
   c. works at a theater

2. He _____ .
   a. works in the manager's office
   b. meets interesting people
   c. hates the work

3. He _____ .
   a. sees the TV producer every day
   b. helps with movie productions
   c. doesn't know how to drive

4. She _____ .
   a. thinks the salary is good
   b. is looking for another job
   c. likes her co-workers

5. He _____ .
   a. works for a magazine
   b. writes about sports news
   c. isn't famous

6. She _____ .
   a. works there only part time
   b. is a waitress
   c. doesn't work anymore

4. Let's Listen 💿

People are talking about their jobs. Which statement is true? Listen and circle the correct answer.

1. He _____ .
    a. does all of his work on the telephone
    b. spends a lot of time talking to people
    c. has worked there a short time
    d. is looking for a new job

2. She _____ .
    a. has a boss
    b. works for a large company
    c. has two big clients
    d. needs more work

3. He _____ .
    a. has a new restaurant
    b. is very busy on the weekends
    c. has very little to do
    d. often does the cooking

4. She _____ .
    a. likes meeting people
    b. doesn't really like traveling
    c. never has a break during a flight
    d. doesn't like the money

Task 2

Listen again. Circle the word that each person uses to describe his or her job.

1. a. hard
   b. quiet
   c. interesting
   d. boring

2. a. creative
   b. boring
   c. easy
   d. unsuccessful

3. a. easy
   b. relaxing
   c. lonely
   d. tough

4. a. difficult
   b. loud
   c. tough
   d. well-paid

Over to You: Talking about jobs

Task 1

Work in small groups. Add two more jobs to the list. Write one advantage and one disadvantage for each job.

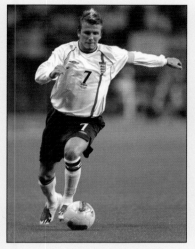
professional soccer player

actress

	Advantages	Disadvantages
1. professional soccer player	_____	_____
2. actor/actress	_____	_____
3. lawyer	_____	_____
4. doctor	_____	_____
5. flight attendant	_____	_____
6. chef	_____	_____
7. _____	_____	_____
8. _____	_____	_____

Task 2

In your small groups, discuss which of the above jobs you would like best and why.

Example: **A:** A professional soccer player meets interesting people.

   B: Right, but they practice a lot.

   C: And they travel all the time.

   D: Yeah, that's true, but…

1. Getting Ready

Match each goal on the left with the correct suggestion on the right. Compare answers with a partner.

1. have a healthier diet _c_

2. tighten stomach muscles ___

3. put on weight ___

4. swim regularly ___

5. get some outdoor exercise ___

a. do lots of sit-ups

b. join a health club with a pool

c. eat less meat and more vegetables

d. lift weights every other day

e. take up jogging

2. Let's Listen

People are talking about New Year's resolutions. What is each person going to do? Listen and circle the correct answer.

1. a. do more exercise
   b. put on weight

2. a. learn to swim
   b. give up smoking

3. a. do more walking
   b. take up jogging

4. a. join a gym
   b. put on weight

5. a. eat less meat
   b. lose some weight

6. a. take up jogging
   b. start doing sit-ups

3. Let's Listen

People are comparing different kinds of exercise. Which kind of exercise does each person prefer now? Listen and check (✓) the correct answer.

1.
  a.   b.

2.
  a.   b.

3.
  a.   b.

4.
  a.   b.

5.
  a.   b.

6.
  a.   b.

Task 2

Listen again. Circle the reason each person likes the kind of exercise he or she does now.

1. **a.** It's not fun.
   b. It's a good place to meet people.

2. **a.** He does it indoors.
   b. He listens to the ocean as he does it.

3. **a.** It's fun.
   b. It's not easy to find a place to play.

4. **a.** It's easy to do it.
   b. She can do it almost anywhere.

5. **a.** It took a short time to learn.
   b. He doesn't usually ride it on busy streets.

6. **a.** It's cheap to do.
   b. It's not as easy as it looks.

4. Let's Listen

People are talking about exercise. Listen and check (✓) the activities they do or do not do now.

	Does	Doesn't do
1. Brandon		
a. swimming	☐	☑
b. jogging	☐	☐
c. bicycling	☐	☐
2. Alicia		
a. jogging	☐	☐
b. aerobics	☐	☐
c. weightlifting	☐	☐
3. Ian		
a. tennis	☐	☐
b. golf	☐	☐
c. weightlifting	☐	☐
4. Krystal		
a. weightlifting	☐	☐
b. swimming	☐	☐
c. jogging	☐	☐

Task 2

Listen again. What sport does each person want to try? Write the correct letter.

1. Brandon ___   **a.** swimming

2. Alicia ___   **b.** tennis

3. Ian ___   **c.** biking

4. Krystal ___   **d.** golf

Over to You: Good ways to keep fit

What are some good ways to keep fit? Add four more ways to the list. Then number them 1 (best), 2 (second best), etc.

___ *ride a bicycle*

___ *work out in health club*

___ _____

___ _____

___ _____

___ _____

Task 2

Work in pairs. Take turns discussing your lists.

Example: **A:** I think the best way to keep fit is to ride a bicycle.

B: Really? I think the best way is to walk up five flights of stairs every day.

Task 3

Work in pairs. Take turns asking and answering the following questions.

1. What do you do now to keep in shape? Do you enjoy it?
2. What activity would you like to try in the future? Why?
3. What activity will you probably never try? Why?

UNIT 11 Invitations

1. Getting Ready

Are these responses used to accept or refuse an invitation? Check (✓) and compare answers with a partner.

	Accept	Refuse
1. Sorry, I'd love to but I have other plans.	☐	☑
2. Thanks. I'd love to.	☐	☐
3. That sounds great. Thanks.	☐	☐
4. Sorry, I don't think I can.	☐	☐
5. Maybe some other time.	☐	☐
6. Sure. That sounds great.	☐	☐
7. I'd love to but...	☐	☐

2. Let's Listen

What is each invitation for? Listen and circle the correct answer.

1. **a.** go to see a movie
   b. go for a snack

2. **a.** go to the health club
   b. go to the beach

3. **a.** see a movie
   b. rent a video

4. **a.** go somewhere before class
   b. go to a coffee shop

5. **a.** come over for dinner
   b. go to a restaurant

6. **a.** rent a video
   b. go to the movies

3. Let's Listen

Task 1

Does each person accept or refuse the invitation? Listen and circle the correct answer.

1. **a.** accept
   b. refuse

2. **a.** accept
   b. refuse

3. **a.** accept
   b. refuse

4. **a.** accept
   b. refuse

5. **a.** accept
   b. refuse

6. **a.** accept
   b. refuse

Task 2

Listen again. Are these statements true or false? Check (✓) the correct answer.

	True	False
1. Mary doesn't like rock music.	☐	☐
2. Jim goes dancing often.	☐	☐
3. Susie has stayed home every night this week.	☐	☐
4. Ben doesn't have tickets to the game.	☐	☐
5. Jenny studies Spanish.	☐	☐
6. Steven only wants to see the match.	☐	☐

4. Let's Listen

Listen to the invitations on Judy's voicemail. Are the statements true or false?
Check (✓) the correct answer.

		True	False
1.	**a.** The invitation is to watch a baseball game.	☐	☑
	b. Friends from school will be there.	☐	☐
	c. They'll go out to eat.	☐	☐
	d. The meeting time is 9:00 p.m.	☐	☐
2.	**a.** The invitation is for lunch on Saturday.	☐	☐
	b. It's a surprise birthday party for Pam.	☐	☐
	c. The meeting time is noon.	☐	☐
	d. Everyone should bring a gift.	☐	☐
3.	**a.** It's an invitation to the theater.	☐	☐
	b. The concert is on Saturday.	☐	☐
	c. An Australian rock group is playing.	☐	☐
	d. They'll have dinner before the concert.	☐	☐
4.	**a.** The invitation is to play tennis.	☐	☐
	b. Some friends are meeting on Sunday afternoon.	☐	☐
	c. The meeting time is 2:00 p.m.	☐	☐
	d. Afterwards, they'll have dinner and see a movie.	☐	☐

Listen again. Should Judy call back or will the person call her again? Circle the correct answer.

1. a. Judy should call.
   b. The caller will call again.

2. a. Judy should call.
   b. The caller will call again.

3. a. Judy should call.
   b. The caller will call again.

4. a. Judy should call.
   b. The caller will call again.

Over to You: Would you like to...?

Move around the class. Invite a different person to do something with you each day of the week. If the person accepts, write his or her name in the calendar below. Use the activities in the box or activities of your own.

go to a movie	go to the art museum	watch a video	go shopping
go out for dinner	go to a concert	go to a ball game	play tennis

Examples: **A:** Kim, would you like to go to a movie on Saturday?

B: Oh, I'd love to. Thanks.

A: Sue, would you like to watch a video at my place tonight?

C: Oh, sorry, I'm not free tonight.

FEBRUARY

15 Monday

Thursday **18**

16 Tuesday

Friday **19**

17 Wednesday

Saturday **20**

Sunday **21**

UNIT 12 Small Talk

1. Getting Ready

Match the questions on the left with the answers on the right. Compare answers with a partner.

1. Are you here on vacation? _c_
2. How long are you staying? ___
3. How do you like it here? ___
4. When did you get here? ___
5. Are you traveling with your family? ___
6. Have you been here before? ___

a. Two weeks ago.
b. No, I'm on my own.
c. No, I'm here on business.
d. Yes, this is my third trip.
e. I'll be here for a month.
f. I really like it.

2. Let's Listen

Where is each conversation taking place? Listen and number the pictures.

A.

B.

C.

D.

E.

F.

3. Let's Listen

Task 1

People are chatting at a party. Are these statements true or false? Listen and check (✓) the correct answer.

	True	False
1. Anne		
a. knows a lot of people at the party.	☐	☐
b. is in town on vacation.	☐	☐
c. is only planning to stay a few days.	☐	☐
d. is sharing an apartment with friends.	☐	☐
2. David		
a. knows a lot of people at the party.	☐	☐
b. is in town on vacation.	☐	☐
c. is staying in a hotel.	☐	☐
d. will go back to Chicago in four days.	☐	☐
3. Debbie		
a. knows a lot of people at the party.	☐	☐
b. is in town on vacation.	☐	☐
c. is staying with her cousin.	☐	☐
d. is planning to stay only a few days.	☐	☐
4. Jim		
a. is staying with a friend.	☐	☐
b. knows a lot of people in town.	☐	☐
c. just started a new job.	☐	☐
d. is planning to stay only a few days.	☐	☐

Task 2

Listen again. Do you think the people will meet again? Circle the correct answer.

1. a. Yes, they probably will meet again.
   b. No, they probably won't meet again.

2. a. Yes, they probably will meet again.
   b. No, they probably won't meet again.

3. a. Yes, they probably will meet again.
   b. No, they probably won't meet again.

4. a. Yes, they probably will meet again.
   b. No, they probably won't meet again.

4. Let's Listen

Task 1

People are talking about their vacations. Listen and number the topics from 1 to 4 in the order they are mentioned.

1. the food ___
   the staff ___
   the people _/_
   the beach ___

2. the taxi ___
   the food ___
   the hotel ___
   the waiters ___

3. the people ___
   the hotel ___
   the bus ___
   the food ___

4. the sightseeing ___
   the buses ___
   the shopping ___
   the people ___

Task 2

Listen again. For each topic, does the person have a positive or negative opinion?
Check (✓) the correct answer.

1.

	Positive	Negative
the people	☐	☐
the beach	☐	☐
the food	☐	☐
the staff	☐	☐

3.

	Positive	Negative
the people	☐	☐
the hotel	☐	☐
the bus	☐	☐
the food	☐	☐

2.

	Positive	Negative
the taxi	☐	☐
the food	☐	☐
the hotel	☐	☐
the waiters	☐	☐

4.

	Positive	Negative
the sightseeing	☐	☐
the buses	☐	☐
the shopping	☐	☐
the people	☐	☐

Over to You: Asking polite questions

In the United States and Canada, when you first meet people it is usually not polite to ask questions about politics, religion, someone's age, or whether they are married.

Task 1

Look at the questions below. Check (✓) the ones that you think are polite.

1. ☐ Do you like sports?
2. ☐ What are your hobbies?
3. ☐ Are you a Christian?
4. ☐ Are you single?
5. ☐ What are you studying?
6. ☐ Why aren't you married?
7. ☐ How old are you?
8. ☐ Do you go skiing?
9. ☐ Do you live in a dormitory?
10. ☐ Where do you go to school?
11. ☐ How much do you weigh?
12. ☐ Do you like sightseeing?

Task 2

Work with a partner and compare your answers. Then ask each other the polite questions.

Task 3

Write three more questions you can ask to make small talk.

1. _____
2. _____
3. _____

Task 4

Ask your partner the questions you wrote in Task 3.

UNIT 13 Hobbies and Pastimes

1. Getting Ready

Who would most enjoy these hobbies and pastimes? Check (✓) your answers and compare them with a partner. There may be more than one answer.

	Young child	Teenager	Adult	Retired person
gardening	☐	☐	☐	☐
cooking	☐	☐	☐	☐
playing in a band	☐	☐	☐	☐
hiking	☐	☐	☐	☐
collecting comic books	☐	☐	☐	☐
playing video games	☐	☐	☐	☐
surfing the Internet	☐	☐	☐	☐

2. Let's Listen 💿

People are talking about hobbies and pastimes. Listen and number the pictures.

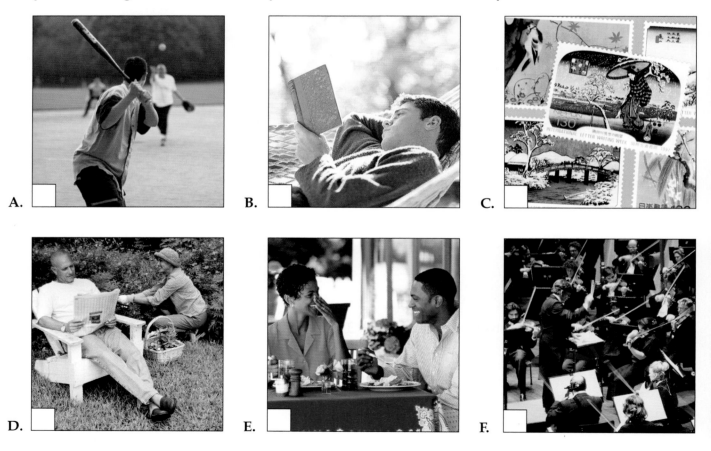

A.

B.

C.

D.

E.

F.

3. Let's Listen 💿

Which activity does each person enjoy doing now? Listen and circle the correct answer.

1. Zachary
   a. playing the guitar
   b. playing in a band
   c. playing the piano

2. Erica
   a. collecting baseball cards
   b. collecting comic books
   c. gardening

3. Bradley
   a. watching videos
   b. hiking
   c. playing video games

4. Evan
   a. collecting stamps
   b. collecting paintings
   c. collecting baseball cards

5. Danielle
   a. painting
   b. writing children's books
   c. reading

6. Marcus
   a. reading the newspaper
   b. playing golf
   c. reading books

Task 2

Listen again. What does each speaker like best about his or her current hobby or pastime? Write the correct letter.

1. Zachary ___
2. Erica ___
3. Bradley ___
4. Evan ___
5. Danielle ___
6. Marcus ___

a. the flowers
b. looking at his collection
c. creating pictures
d. the people
e. looking at the blue sky
f. making great friends

4. Let's Listen

Task 1

People are talking about their interests. Listen and check (✓) two suitable hobbies for each person.

1. Scott
   - ☐ surfing the Internet
   - ☐ gardening
   - ☐ birdwatching
   - ☐ hiking

2. Christine
   - ☐ music
   - ☐ birdwatching
   - ☐ gardening
   - ☐ cooking

3. Joe
   - ☐ sports
   - ☐ hiking
   - ☐ music
   - ☐ surfing the Internet

4. Amy
   - ☐ hiking
   - ☐ reading
   - ☐ sports
   - ☐ surfing the Internet

Task 2

Listen again. What is one activity each person likes doing? Circle the correct answer.

1. a. enjoying nature
   b. hiking
   c. sitting in a coffee shop

2. a. birdwatching
   b. visiting the countryside
   c. getting together with friends

3. a. surfing the Internet
   b. exercising
   c. playing the guitar

4. a. learning something new
   b. going to parties
   c. working out at the gym

Over to You: Do you like...?

Check (✓) the hobbies and pastimes you enjoy.

Hobbies/Pastimes	You	Your partner
1. taking photos	☐	☐
2. reading comic books	☐	☐
3. talking with friends on the phone	☐	☐
4. listening to music	☐	☐
5. skiing or snowboarding	☐	☐
6. going to the movies	☐	☐
7. watching videos at home	☐	☐
8. playing baseball	☐	☐
9. playing computer games	☐	☐
10. playing the piano	☐	☐
11. shopping	☐	☐
12. doing arts and crafts	☐	☐
13. surfing the Internet	☐	☐
14. cooking	☐	☐
15. driving	☐	☐

Task 2

Work in pairs. Take turns asking each other questions. Check (✓) the things in the chart above that your partner likes.

Example: **A:** Do you like ... ?

           B: It's okay. / Yeah. I love it. / No, not much. / I've never tried it.

Task 3

Work in pairs. Take turns asking each other questions about the hobbies and pastimes that are checked (✓) above. Find out *why*, *how often*, *when*, and *where* your partner does the activities.

UNIT 14 Shopping Problems

1. Getting Ready

Have you ever had these problems? Check (✓) your answers and compare them with a partner.

You bought something that _____ .

- ☐ shrank when you washed it
- ☐ had a missing part
- ☐ was the wrong size
- ☐ didn't work
- ☐ changed color when you washed it
- ☐ was damaged
- ☐ was poorly made
- ☐ other: _____

2. Let's Listen

Which item did each person receive? Listen and check (✓) the correct answer.

1.
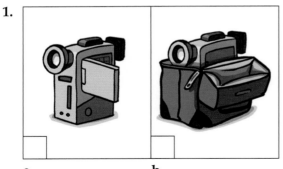

   a.   b.

2.
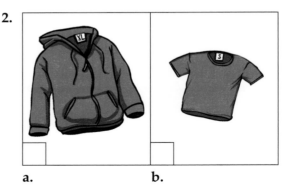

   a.   b.

3.
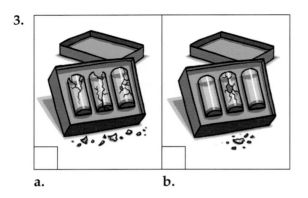

   a.   b.

4.
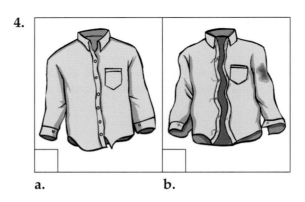

   a.   b.

3. Let's Listen 📀

Task 1

Customers are describing a problem. Listen and circle the correct answer.

1. **a.** He needs a bigger size.
   b. He needs a smaller size.

2. **a.** The shoes are too small.
   b. The shoes are damaged.

3. **a.** The lock is missing.
   b. The lock isn't working.

4. **a.** The band is too big.
   b. The band is broken.

5. **a.** The shirt has shrunk.
   b. The buttons have come off the shirt.

6. **a.** The back doesn't close.
   b. The shutter is broken.

Task 2

Listen again. Are these statements true or false? Check (✓) the correct answer.

	True	False
1. The clerk asks the customer to come back tomorrow.	☐	☐
2. The clerk asks for the receipt.	☐	☐
3. The customer has to bring the briefcase back in a few days.	☐	☐
4. The customer should call the clerk by tonight.	☐	☐
5. The clerk asks the customer to fill out a form.	☐	☐
6. The customer needs to show the clerk the guarantee.	☐	☐

4. Let's Listen

Task 1

People are talking about shopping. Listen and circle the correct information about each person.

1. a. She enjoyed going to the store.
   b. There were good bargains.
   c. She bought many things.

2. a. He didn't like the clothes he bought.
   b. He didn't buy much.
   c. Most of the things he bought were good.

3. a. The camera cost nearly $150.
   b. The camera doesn't work well.
   c. The camera cost more in a different store.

4. a. She thought the prices were reasonable.
   b. She bargained when she bought them.
   c. Her friend got things for a higher price.

Task 2

Listen again. What phrase completes each statement? Write the correct letter.

1. Next time, she won't ___
2. Next time, he'll save his money and ___
3. Next time, he'll spend more time ___
4. Next time, she'll be sure to ___

a. comparing prices before buying something.
b. go shopping during a big sale.
c. bargain.
d. wait for the sales at home.

Over to You: What seems to be the problem?

Task 1

What are some things you can buy in a department store? Write five more things.

1. _a pair of shoes_
2. _____
3. _____
4. _____
5. _____
6. _____

Task 2

Work in pairs. Student A is a salesperson in a department store.
Student B is a customer. Practice the conversation below.

A: Hi. What seems to be the problem?

B: Well, it's this (1) <u>shirt</u>. I bought it here (2) <u>yesterday</u>.

A: And what's the problem?

B: It (3) <u>is the wrong size</u>.

A: Oh, really? Well, (4) <u>we can replace it</u>.

Task 3

Work in pairs. Have three more conversations like the one in Task 2.
Use this information.

(1) dress	pair of pants	skirt
(2) last week	last weekend	two days ago
(3) has a hole in it	is broken/damaged	is missing a part
(4) we can get a new one for you	you can return it	you can exchange it

Task 4

Work in pairs. Take turns role-playing the situation in Task 2. Use your
own information.

1. Getting Ready

Which numbers in a hotel do you call for the following services? Write the numbers next to the services. Compare answers with a partner.

HOTEL SERVICES

Front Desk
Dial 5

Housekeeping
Dial 10

Laundry
Dial 9

Operator
Dial 7

Bell Captain
Dial 6

Room Service
Dial 15

1. To order a meal in your room, dial _15_.

2. To get clothes dry-cleaned, dial ___.

3. To get help carrying your bags, dial ___.

4. To get your room cleaned, dial ___.

5. To make a long-distance call, dial ___.

6. To check if you have received mail, dial ___.

2. Let's Listen

People are making calls from their hotel rooms. Who is each person calling? Listen and circle the correct answer.

1. **a.** laundry
   b. room service

2. **a.** operator
   b. bell captain

3. **a.** housekeeping
   b. room service

4. **a.** bell captain
   b. laundry

5. **a.** front desk
   b. room service

6. **a.** operator
   b. housekeeping

3. Let's Listen

Task 1

**People are talking to a hotel receptionist. What does each person want to do?
Listen and circle the correct answer.**

1. a. leave a message
   b. check for messages
   c. pick up mail

2. a. move to a bigger room
   b. move to a quieter room
   c. move to a smoking room

3. a. arrange for a taxi for the morning
   b. arrange for a taxi for tonight
   c. learn to set the alarm clock

4. a. drive to a restaurant
   b. eat something without meat
   c. eat in the restaurant

Task 2

Listen again. Are these statements true or false? Check (✓) the correct answer.

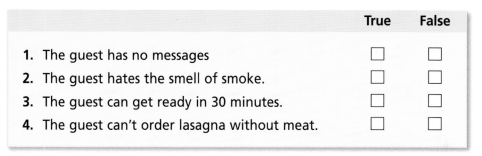

	True	False
1. The guest has no messages	☐	☐
2. The guest hates the smell of smoke.	☐	☐
3. The guest can get ready in 30 minutes.	☐	☐
4. The guest can't order lasagna without meat.	☐	☐

4. Let's Listen

Task 1

People are talking about the hotels they are staying in. Listen and check (✓) their opinions about each hotel.

1.

	Good	Not good
the restaurant	☐	✓
the service	☐	☐
the room	☐	☐
the rates	☐	☐

2.

	Good	Not good
the restaurant	☐	☐
the service	☐	☐
the room	☐	☐
the rates	☐	☐

3.

	Good	Not good
the restaurant	☐	☐
the service	☐	☐
the room	☐	☐
the rates	☐	☐

4.

	Good	Not good
the restaurants	☐	☐
the service	☐	☐
the room	☐	☐
the rates	☐	☐

Task 2

Listen again. What phrase completes each statement? Write the correct letter.

1. The hotel should have one restaurant that's ___
2. The hotel should buy ___
3. The hotel should get ___
4. The hotel should have at least one ___

a. just for adults.
b. a new manager.
c. cheap, casual restaurant.
d. softer mattresses.

Over to You: Problems in a hotel

Task 1

Work in pairs. A hotel receptionist and a hotel guest are talking. Number the ten sentences in A and B to make a conversation. Then take turns practicing it.

A

—— Certainly. How many do you want?

—— 1610. Someone will be right up.
Have a good day.

_1_ Can I help you?

—— Two. Got it. I'll send them right away.
Oh, and what's your room number?

—— I'm sorry. I'll send someone right away.
Is there anything else I can do for you?

B

—— I'm in 1610.

—— Yes, please. Can I get some extra towels?

—— Thanks. You, too.

_2_ Yes. My room is freezing.
I think the air conditioner is broken.

—— Two, please.

Task 2

Choose two of the situations. Write a conversation with your partner, then practice it.

1. There's no coffee for the coffeemaker.
2. The people in the next room are too noisy.
3. You want to order a continental breakfast for tomorrow morning.
4. You need a wake-up call for 6:30.

1. Getting Ready

Match each kind of movie on the left with the best description on the right. Compare answers with a partner.

1. romance _b_

2. western ___

3. horror ___

4. action ___

5. science fiction ___

6. comedy ___

a. A movie about events that take place in the future or in other parts of the universe.

b. A movie that tells a love story.

c. A movie about life in the west of the United States in the nineteenth century.

d. A movie that tries to scare the audience.

e. A movie that tries to make people laugh.

f. A movie with a fast-moving story that is full of danger and excitement.

2. Let's Listen

People are talking about movies. What kind of movie does each person describe? Listen and circle the correct answer.

1. a. science fiction
   b. action

2. a. action
   b. comedy

3. a. horror
   b. western

4. a. science fiction
   b. comedy

5. a. romance
   b. western

6. a. action
   b. science fiction

3. Let's Listen

Task 1

People are calling for information about movies. What type of movie is it?
Listen and write the correct letter.

a. western　　**b.** comedy　　**c.** horror　　**d.** action　　**e.** science fiction　　**f.** romance

1.
> **CINEMA 1**
>
> title: *Die Harder: The Final Conflict*
>
> type: ___

4.
> **CINEMA 4**
>
> title: *Cowboy's Run*
>
> type: ___

2.
> **CINEMA 2**
>
> title: *Party Animal*
>
> type: ___

5.
> **CINEMA 5**
>
> title: *Space Children*
>
> type: ___

3.
> **CINEMA 3**
>
> title: *Dreams*
>
> type: ___

6.
> **CINEMA 6**
>
> title: *Monster Party*
>
> type: ___

Task 2

Listen again. Write the show times.

Cinema 1　*2:30, 4:45, 7:30, 10:00*

Cinema 2　_____

Cinema 3　_____

Cinema 4　_____

Cinema 5　_____

Cinema 6　_____

4. Let's Listen

Task 1

People are talking about movies. What did they like or not like about each movie?
Listen and check (✓) the correct answers.

1.

	Liked	Didn't like
the story	☐	☐
the acting	☐	☐
the ending	☐	☐
the music	☐	☐

3.

	Liked	Didn't like
the story	☐	☐
the acting	☐	☐
the ending	☐	☐
the music	☐	☐

2.

	Liked	Didn't like
the story	☐	☐
the acting	☐	☐
the ending	☐	☐
the music	☐	☐

4.

	Liked	Didn't like
the story	☐	☐
the acting	☐	☐
the ending	☐	☐
the music	☐	☐

Task 2

Listen again. Does each person recommend the movie or not? Check (✓) the correct answer.

1. ☐ yes   2. ☐ yes   3. ☐ yes   4. ☐ yes
   ☐ no   ☐ no   ☐ no   ☐ no

Over to You: Would you like to go to a movie?

Task 1

Work in pairs. Role-play. Student A invites Student B to a movie tonight. Student B answers Student A's questions, using the information from the pictures above.

Example: **A:** Hey, would you like to go to a movie tonight?

B: Yeah, I'd love to.

A: What's showing?

B: Well, *Red Windmill* is showing at 6:45 and 9:45.

A: *Red Windmill*? That's a musical, isn't it?

B: Yes, it is.

A: Great. I love musicals. Who's in it?

B: Nicole Codfish.

A: Oh, she's really good.

B: Yeah, she is.

A: Let's meet at 6:30.

B: Okay. See you then.

Task 2

Work in pairs. Take turns inviting each other to a movie of your choice.

UNIT 17 Fears

1. Getting Ready

Are you afraid of any of the things below? Check (✓) your answers and compare them with a partner.

	Yes	No
heights	☐	☐
riding roller coasters	☐	☐
spiders	☐	☐
snakes	☐	☐
mice	☐	☐
cockroaches	☐	☐
bats	☐	☐
small spaces	☐	☐
scuba diving	☐	☐
flying on airplanes	☐	☐
driving on freeways	☐	☐
other: _____	☐	☐

2. Let's Listen

What is happening in these pictures? Listen and number the pictures.

A.

B.

C.

D.

E.

F.

3. Let's Listen

Task 1

People are describing fears. Has each speaker's fear decreased over the years?
Listen and check (✓) the correct answer.

1. ☐ yes   4. ☐ yes
   ☐ no   ☐ no

2. ☐ yes   5. ☐ yes
   ☐ no   ☐ no

3. ☐ yes   6. ☐ yes
   ☐ no   ☐ no

Task 2

Listen again. Circle the correct statement.

1. a. She learned to fly a plane.
   b. An airplane engineer explained how
      planes stay in the air.

2. a. A snake tried to bite her while she was hiking.
   b. A snake bit her at the zoo.

3. a. His friend hated spiders.
   b. He studied spiders in college.

4. a. He learned how to swim.
   b. He went to the beach often when he was a kid.

5. a. His friend was in a car accident.
   b. He was in a car accident.

6. a. She loved going to the zoo when she was a kid.
   b. She was given a puppy for her birthday.

4. Let's Listen

People are talking about their fears. Is each statement true or false?
Listen and check (✓) the correct answer.

	True	False
1. **a.** He has never had bad experiences in elevators.	☐	☐
b. He doesn't like the feeling of not being able to get out.	☐	☐
2. **a.** She is afraid of waves.	☐	☐
b. She likes pools because there are lots of people around.	☐	☐
3. **a.** She is afraid of dogs and cats.	☐	☐
b. She has been bitten by a dog.	☐	☐
4. **a.** He doesn't mind looking out of windows on high floors.	☐	☐
b. He doesn't like flying.	☐	☐

Listen again. What problem does the fear cause for each person? Circle the correct answer.

1. **a.** He can never use elevators.
   b. He hates using stairs.
   c. He has to use the elevator with someone else.

2. **a.** She can't swim in a pool.
   b. She can't swim in the ocean.
   c. She can't be in crowds.

3. **a.** She can't visit people with big dogs.
   b. She can't visit people with any animals.
   c. She can't visit people with any dogs.

4. **a.** He can't work in a tall building.
   b. He never travels.
   c. He can't do some fun things with his kids.

Over to You: Which animals are you afraid of?

Work in groups of three. Which animals are you afraid of? Which ones would you like to keep as pets? Discuss your answers using the conversations and the words in the box below.

cute
unusual
slimy
soft
furry
dangerous
sharp
gentle
ugly
smelly

rat

lamb

lizard

lion cub

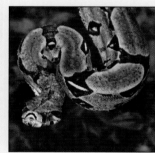
snake

rabbit

Examples: **A:** Which ones are you afraid of?

B: I'm afraid of… / I can't stand…

C: Why?

B: Well, because…

A: Which ones would you like as a pet?

B: I'd like…

C: Why?

B: Because…

UNIT 18 Telephone Messages

1. Getting Ready

Do you use the telephone often? Fill in the information below. Compare answers with a partner.

Average number of telephone calls I make a day: _____

People I call most often: _____

2. Let's Listen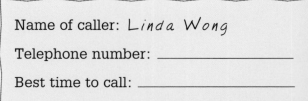

Listen to the messages on Susie's voicemail. Complete the information about each call.

1.
Name of caller: *David*

Telephone number: _____

Best time to call: *after* _____

2.
Name of caller: *Mary*

Telephone number: _____

Best time to call: *between* ___ *and* ___

3.
Name of caller: *Peter Rogers*

Telephone number: _____

Best time to call: *between* ___ *and* ___

4.
Name of caller: *Linda Wong*

Telephone number: _____

Best time to call: _____

3. Let's Listen

Task 1

Listen to these messages on Andre's voicemail. Circle the correct message.

1. a. Pick up the car on Tuesday morning.
   b. Pick up the car on Friday afternoon.

2. a. ABC Express will deliver a package tomorrow.
   b. ABC Express delivered a package today.

3. a. Susan is inviting Andre to a party on Saturday.
   b. Susan is telling Andre she will come to his party.

4. a. The CD has arrived.
   b. The CD hasn't arrived yet.

5. a. Kathy cannot go to dinner.
   b. Kathy can go to dinner after work.

6. a. Dr. Costello can give Andre a dental appointment on Thursday.
   b. Dr. Costello can give Andre a dental appointment on Tuesday

Task 2

Listen again. Does the caller want Andre to call back or will the caller telephone again later? Check (✓) the correct answer.

	Andre should return the call.	The caller will telephone Andre.
1.	☐	☐
2.	☐	☐
3.	☐	☐
4.	☐	☐
5.	☐	☐
6.	☐	☐

4. Let's Listen 💿

Task 1

Daniel is listening to messages on his voicemail at work. Is each statement true or false?
Listen and check (✓) the correct answer.

		True	False
1.	a. The message is from an airline company.	☐	☑
	b. The flights are confirmed.	☐	☐
	c. Free transportation to the hotel is available.	☐	☐
	d. The driver should not be tipped.	☐	☐
2.	a. The message is from the mailroom.	☐	☐
	b. The package is waiting.	☐	☐
	c. The mailroom will deliver the package.	☐	☐
	d. He received a letter.	☐	☐
3.	a. The invitation is for dinner.	☐	☐
	b. He wants to go to a Mexican restaurant.	☐	☐
	c. He suggests a boat trip after the meal.	☐	☐
	d. He will call again later.	☐	☐
4.	a. The shirts can be picked up now.	☐	☐
	b. The store is open until 9:00 p.m.	☐	☐
	c. The cost is $29.	☐	☐
	d. You can pay by cash or credit card.	☐	☐

Task 2

Listen again. What is each caller's telephone number? Write the answers.

1. Mary _____

2. Peter _ext._____

3. Frank _____

4. Mrs. Lee _____

Over to You: Leaving a message

Task 1

Work in pairs. Plan two messages to leave on someone's voicemail. Write your messages in the spaces provided. Use the list below or your own ideas.

You borrowed something and lost it.

Give the reason you have to miss a big test or work.

You want to borrow something.

You need the money you lent someone.

You want the person to do something for you.

You want to ask a friend to do something with you.

Your messages

Message for _____

Message: _____

_____

_____

_____

Message for _____

Message: _____

_____

_____

_____

Task 2

Stand back-to-back with your partner. Take turns reading each of your messages. Write what your partner tells you.

Your partner's messages

Message for _____

Message: _____

_____

_____

_____

Message for _____

Message: _____

_____

_____

_____

UNIT 19 Touring a City

1. Getting Ready

What do you do when you visit a new city? Check (✓) your answers and compare them with a partner.

- ☐ visit museums
- ☐ visit churches or temples
- ☐ take a bus tour
- ☐ try local food
- ☐ go to the zoo
- ☐ buy souvenirs
- ☐ go shopping
- ☐ attend local cultural events
- ☐ other: _____

2. Let's Listen

People are visiting a city. Where are they? Listen and number the pictures.

A. ☐

B. ☐

C. ☐

D. ☐

E. ☐

F. ☐

3. Let's Listen 💿

Tour guides are describing some of the things people will see or do on a tour.
Listen and circle the correct answers.

1. **a.** take pictures of the stars' houses
   b. see Marilyn Monroe's house
   c. see Joe DiMaggio's house
   d. see James Dean's house
   e. see Arnold Schwarzenegger's house

2. **a.** go to the Empire State Building
   b. visit the Statue of Liberty
   c. take a taxi uptown
   d. have a picnic in Central Park
   e. go ice skating at Rockefeller Center

3. **a.** hike in the mountains
   b. visit a market
   c. eat food at the market
   d. go inside a temple
   e. touch the statues

4. **a.** see a baseball game
   b. go to a museum
   c. see the museum's most famous painting
   d. take a boat ride
   e. eat pizza with Al Capone

Task 2

Listen again. Are these statements true or false? Check (✓) the correct answer.

	True	False
1. People can take pictures of the stars' houses.	☐	☐
2. People can buy a photo of the ice rink.	☐	☐
3. People can buy many kinds of souvenirs.	☐	☐
4. People can't buy tickets for any baseball game.	☐	☐

4. Let's Listen

Task 1

People are talking about the tours they took. What was good or bad about each tour? Listen and check (✓) the correct answers.

1.	Good	Not good
the itinerary	☐	☐
the guide	☐	☐
the food	☐	☐
the price	☐	☐

3.	Good	Not good
the itinerary	☐	☐
the guide	☐	☐
the food	☐	☐
the price	☐	☐

2.	Good	Not good
the itinerary	☐	☐
the guide	☐	☐
the food	☐	☐
the price	☐	☐

4.	Good	Not good
the itinerary	☐	☐
the guide	☐	☐
the food	☐	☐
the price	☐	☐

Task 2

Listen again. Would each person recommend the tour? Check (✓) the correct answer.

1. ☐ yes   2. ☐ yes   3. ☐ yes   4. ☐ yes
   ☐ no   ☐ no   ☐ no   ☐ no

Over to You: You have visitors

Task 1

Work in pairs. Friends from abroad are visiting your city or hometown for a few days. Write three things they should do or places they should visit. Discuss your suggestions with your partner.

Name of city: _____

Suggestions	Reasons
1. _____	_____
2. _____	_____
3. _____	_____

Example: **Honolulu**

A: I think they should go to Waikiki Beach.

B: Why?

A: Because it's beautiful there and you can go swimming.

B: Do you think they should walk up Diamond Head?

A: Well, maybe, but it takes a long time.

Task 2

Now, think about some place you've been. What did you do there? Why? Fill in the chart below. Then discuss what you wrote with a partner.

Name of city: _____

Things you did / Places you saw	Reasons
1. _____	_____
2. _____	_____
3. _____	_____

UNIT 20 Airports

1. Getting Ready

Match each activity on the left with the correct place on the right.
Compare answers with a partner.

1. freshen up after a flight _d_
2. board a flight ___
3. meet a friend arriving on a flight ___
4. get flight information ___
5. change money ___
6. pick up suitcases after a flight ___
7. buy a magazine ___
8. take a bus to a different terminal ___

a. arrivals area
b. baggage-claim area
c. newsstand
d. restroom
e. shuttle bus stop
f. departure gate
g. currency exchange
h. arrival and departure board

2. Let's Listen

Where do these people want to go? Listen and check (✓) the correct picture.

1.

a.   b.

2.

a.   b.

3.

a.   b.

4.

a.   b.

3. Let's Listen

Task 1

What are these people talking about? Listen and circle the correct answer.

1. a. directions
   b. flight insurance
   c. flight information

2. a. ticketing information
   b. a flight departure time
   c. a flight arrival time

3. a. directions to the hotel
   b. hotel prices
   c. car rentals

4. a. customs and immigration
   b. shopping
   c. ATM machines

INFORMATION

Task 2

Listen again. Are these statements true or false? Check (✓) the correct answer.

		True	False
1.	a. She needs to find Terminal B.	☐	☐
	b. The bus leaves in twenty minutes.	☐	☐
	c. She doesn't need to buy a ticket.	☐	☐
2.	a. The clerk doesn't help the man.	☐	☐
	b. The flight arrival time will appear later.	☐	☐
	c. The man should check the monitor in 50 minutes.	☐	☐
3.	a. There are maps on Level 1.	☐	☐
	b. She plans to drive to the hotel.	☐	☐
	c. The hotel is near the airport.	☐	☐
4.	a. There aren't a lot of stores to choose from.	☐	☐
	b. She doesn't have to go through customs and immigration first.	☐	☐
	c. She can't use credit cards.	☐	☐

4. Let's Listen

People are talking about airports in different cities. Listen and check (✓) the correct answers.

1.

	Good	Not good
the location	✓	☐
the transportation	☐	☐
the facilities	☐	☐
the check-in	☐	☐

3.

	Good	Not good
the location	☐	☐
the transportation	☐	☐
the facilities	☐	☐
the check-in	☐	☐

2.

	Good	Not good
the location	☐	☐
the transportation	☐	☐
the facilities	☐	☐
the check-in	☐	☐

4.

	Good	Not good
the location	☐	☐
the transportation	☐	☐
the facilities	☐	☐
the check-in	☐	☐

Task 2

Listen again. What phrase completes each statement? Write the correct letter.

1. The airport should put in ___
2. The airport needs to add ___
3. There should be ___
4. The city needs to build ___

a. some more check-in counters.
b. some stores and cafes.
c. a new airport closer to the city.
d. a bus service into town.

Over to You: Getting around the airport

Task 1

Look at these questions people often ask at airports. Add three more questions of your own.

1. Excuse me. Where can I change money?

2. Is there a taxi stand near here?

3. How much is the bus to the city?

4. Where's the arrival area?

5. Where's the duty-free area?

6. _____

   _____

7. _____

   _____

8. _____

   _____

Task 2

Work in pairs. Imagine you are in an airport. How would you answer each of the questions above?

1. _____

2. _____

3. _____

4. _____

5. _____

6. _____

7. _____

8. _____

Task 3

Move around the class. Practice asking and answering the questions in Task 1.

UNIT 21 Hotels

1. Getting Ready

What do you usually do when you check into a hotel? Check (✓) your answers and compare them with a partner.

☐ show some identification

☐ give your credit card number

☐ pay for the room in advance

☐ pay a deposit

☐ show a letter from your company or school

☐ fill out a registration card

☐ show your airline tickets

☐ give a confirmation number

☐ other: _____

2. Let's Listen

People are checking into a hotel. What do they have to do? Listen and circle the correct answers.

1. a. fill out a form
   b. show a driver's license
   c. show a passport
   d. pay a deposit
   e. give the receptionist his credit card

2. a. give the confirmation number
   b. show a driver's license
   c. show a passport
   d. pay cash for the room
   e. leave a deposit

3. a. spell her name
   b. show a driver's license
   c. show an airline ticket
   d. fill out a registration form
   e. sign a card

4. a. show a company ID
   b. show a passport
   c. give the receptionist her credit card
   d. fill out a card
   e. leave a deposit

3. Let's Listen

What kind of room does each guest want? Listen and check (✓) the correct answers.

1. ☐ single   ☐ double
   ☐ standard   ☐ deluxe
   ☐ non-smoking   ☐ smoking

2. ☐ single   ☐ double
   ☐ standard   ☐ deluxe
   ☐ non-smoking   ☐ smoking

3. ☐ single   ☐ double
   ☐ standard   ☐ deluxe
   ☐ non-smoking   ☐ smoking

4. ☐ single   ☐ double
   ☐ standard   ☐ deluxe
   ☐ non-smoking   ☐ smoking

Task 2

Listen again. What else does each guest request? Circle the correct answer.

1. **a.** where to find public transportation
   b. a room away from the street

2 **a.** a fruit basket
   b. a wake-up call

3. **a.** an iron
   b. some clothes

4. **a.** coffee and sandwiches
   b. coffee and a salad

4. Let's Listen

Task 1

People are discussing their rooms. Listen and check (✓) the correct information.

1.

	Good	Not good
the size	☐	☐
the bathroom	☐	☐
the view	☐	☐
the facilities	☐	☐

3.

	Good	Not good
the size	☐	☐
the bathroom	☐	☐
the view	☐	☐
the facilities	☐	☐

2.

	Good	Not good
the size	☐	☐
the bathroom	☐	☐
the view	☐	☐
the facilities	☐	☐

4.

	Good	Not good
the size	☐	☐
the bathroom	☐	☐
the view	☐	☐
the facilities	☐	☐

Task 2

Listen again. What did each guest complain about? Circle the correct answer.

1. **a.** that there was nothing in the refrigerator
   b. that the TV and fax machine did not work

2. **a.** the size of the bathroom
   b. the mattress

3. **a.** the view from the window
   b. the heat in the room

4. **a.** the shower
   b. the stereo

Over to You: I'd like to check in, please.

Task 1

Person B is a guest checking into a hotel. Person A is a hotel receptionist. Fill in the blanks in Person A's part with questions from the box below.

Will you be paying with cash or a credit card?   Do you have a reservation?
Okay. Can you sign this, please?   Can I have your name, please?   Hello. Can I help you?

A: (1) _____

B: Yes, I'd like to check in, please.

A: (2) _____

B: Yes, I do.

A: (3) _____

B: Certainly. It's Mr. Johnson.

A: Okay, Mr. Johnson. That's a single, non-smoking room for two nights?

B: Yes, that's right.

A: (4) _____

B: Cash.

A: (5) _____

B: Sure.

A: Thanks. Here's your key. Room 2004.

B: Thank you very much.

Task 2

Work in pairs. Practice the conversation in Task 1.

Task 3

Work in pairs. Practice the conversation in Task 1, using your own information. Fill out the registration form below.

HOTEL ST. GEORGE

Name _____

Type of room _____

Length of stay _____

Form of payment _____

_____
Signature

UNIT 22 Traffic

1. Getting Ready

Match the pictures with the descriptions. Write the correct letter next to each description. Compare your answers with a partner.

1. Road repair ___

2. Two cars in a collision ___

3. Traffic congestion on a freeway _A_

4. Traffic moving smoothly on a freeway ___

A.   B.   C.   D.

2. Let's Listen

People are making announcements about traffic conditions. Listen and number the pictures.

A.    B.    C.

D.    E.    F.

3. Let's Listen

Task 1

These people have to go somewhere. How will each person get there? Listen and circle the correct answer.

1. **a.** by bus
   b. by car
   c. by bicycle

2. **a.** by car
   b. by bus
   c. by subway

3. **a.** by taxi
   b. by car
   c. by bus

4. **a.** by car
   b. by bus
   c. by taxi

5. **a.** by car
   b. by taxi and subway
   c. by subway and on foot

6. **a.** by car
   b. by bike
   c. by bus

Task 2

Listen again. Are these statements true or false? Check (✓) the correct answer.

	True	False
1. There is a big baseball game today.	☐	☐
2. There is a traffic jam on the freeway.	☐	☐
3. Taxis usually don't come very quickly.	☐	☐
4. Kevin lives close to Harry.	☐	☐
5. The traffic is backing up because a traffic light is broken.	☐	☐
6. The weather is not so good.	☐	☐

4. Let's Listen 💿

Task 1

People are describing solutions to traffic problems in their cities. What did each city do?
Listen and circle the correct answer.

1. **a.** They improved the quality of buses.
   b. They raised bus fares on weekends.
   c. They lowered taxi fares.

2. **a.** They built more parking garages.
   b. They made drivers pay a daily fee.
   c. They kept all cars out of the city center.

3. **a.** They made many streets downtown one-way.
   b. They made new lanes for cars to use.
   c. They made a law that people can drive downtown
   every day if they have a special pass.

4. **a.** They did not allow people to ride a bicycle downtown.
   b. They made a rule that there must be at least three
   people in a car to go downtown.
   c. They bought new buses that don't create pollution.

Task 2

Listen again. What problem did each city have? Write the correct letter.

1. ___   **a.** The traffic moved too slowly.
2. ___   **b.** There weren't enough parking spaces.
3. ___   **c.** The public transportation wasn't very good.
4. ___   **d.** The air pollution in the city needed to be lowered.

Over to You: Transportation survey

Task 1

Complete this transportation survey.

1. **How often do you take public transportation?**
   - ☐ every day
   - ☐ once or twice a week
   - ☐ once or twice a month
   - ☐ other: _____

2. **What kinds of public transportation do you use?**
   - ☐ train
   - ☐ bus
   - ☐ taxi
   - ☐ subway
   - ☐ other: _____

3. **What do you think of public transportation where you live?**
   - ☐ very good
   - ☐ okay
   - ☐ needs improvement

4. **What do you think of the price of public transportation?**
   - ☐ too expensive
   - ☐ reasonable
   - ☐ inexpensive

Task 2

Work in pairs. Ask and answer the questions in the survey. Explain your answers.

Example: **A:** How often do you take public transportation?

          B: Every day. I don't drive, so I have to take the subway.

Task 3

Ask your partner the following questions.

1. What's your favorite form of transportation? Why?
2. What's your least favorite form of transportation? Why?

UNIT 23 Roommates

1. Getting Ready

What are some important qualities of a roommate? Check (✓) the four most important qualities and add another of your own. Compare answers with a partner.

- ☐ good-tempered
- ☐ good cook
- ☐ doesn't snore
- ☐ reliable
- ☐ studious
- ☐ sociable
- ☐ thoughtful
- ☐ sense of humor
- ☐ quiet
- ☐ talkative
- ☐ neat
- ☐ considerate
- ☐ other: _____

2. Let's Listen

People are talking about their roommates. Listen and circle the two words that best describe each person.

1. **a.** considerate
   b. messy
   c. helpful
   d. unreliable

2. **a.** unfriendly
   b. talkative
   c. studious
   d. generous

3. **a.** messy
   b. studious
   c. sociable
   d. humorous

4. **a.** unreliable
   b. inconsiderate
   c. neat
   d. helpful

5. **a.** neat
   b. sociable
   c. considerate
   d. studious

6. **a.** lazy
   b. quiet
   c. studious
   d. bad-tempered

3. Let's Listen

Task 1

People are comparing their new roommate with their old roommate. Which one does each person prefer? Listen and check (✓) the correct answer.

	The new one	The old one
1.	☐	☐
2.	☐	☐
3.	☐	☐
4.	☐	☐
5.	☐	☐
6.	☐	☐

Task 2

Listen again. What word or phrase describes each person's favorite roommate? Write the correct letter.

1. ___   **a.** considerate
2. ___   **b.** humorous
3. ___   **c.** neat and clean
4. ___   **d.** thoughtful
5. ___   **e.** not too talkative
6. ___   **f.** friendly and happy

4. Let's Listen

Task 1

People left voicemails for their roommates. What do they want their roommates to do? Listen and circle the correct answer.

1. **a.** make the bed
   b. lend him a book
   c. bring him a book

2. **a.** invite her friends over
   b. buy some snacks
   c. make some snacks

3. **a.** call his parents
   b. make restaurant reservations
   c. clean the living room

4. **a.** buy some food
   b. clean the room
   c. empty out the refrigerator

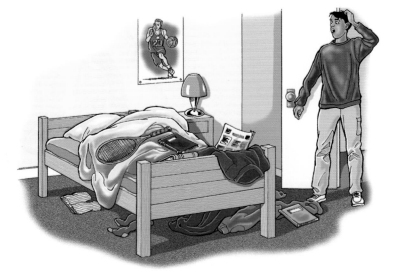

Task 2

Listen again. Are these statements true or false? Check (✓) the correct answer.

	True	False
1. Ted did not make his bed this morning.	☐	☐
2. Margaret invited friends over to play games.	☐	☐
3. John is going to buy dinner for Ken.	☐	☐
4. Carrie forgot to clean the apartment.	☐	☐

Over to You: Roommate survey

Task 1

Imagine you want to find a roommate. Read these questions. Put a check (✓) under "You" for the questions you answer with Yes.

	You	Classmate 1	Classmate 2
Do you like to get up late?	☐	☐	☐
Do you smoke?	☐	☐	☐
Do you snore?	☐	☐	☐
Are you neat?	☐	☐	☐
Do you like cooking?	☐	☐	☐
Do you like parties?	☐	☐	☐
Are you studious?	☐	☐	☐
Do you like loud music?	☐	☐	☐
Are you talkative?	☐	☐	☐
Do you have any pets?	☐	☐	☐
Do you like to stay up late?	☐	☐	☐
Are you lazy?	☐	☐	☐
Do you talk on the phone a lot?	☐	☐	☐
other: _____	☐	☐	☐

Task 2

Add your own question to the list in the chart above.

Task 3

Move around the class and interview two other students. Check (✓) their Yes answers in the chart.

Task 4

Discuss your chart with two different classmates. Who is like you? Who isn't like you? Use your chart and your classmates' answers to decide which classmates would be good roommates. Explain your answers.

UNIT 24 Travel

1. Getting Ready

Which of these have ever happened to you on vacation? Check (✓) your answers and compare them with a partner.

	Yes	No
You missed a flight.	☐	☐
Someone stole your money.	☐	☐
You lost your wallet.	☐	☐
You lost your passport.	☐	☐
Your bags didn't arrive.	☐	☐
You got sick.	☐	☐
You ran out of money.	☐	☐

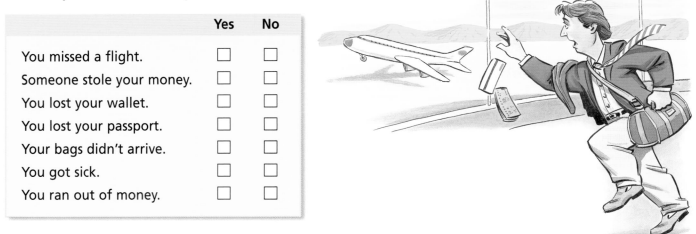

2. Let's Listen

Cindy is talking about her vacation. Listen and number the pictures.

A.

B.

C.

D.

E.

F.

3. Let's Listen

Task 1

People are calling home while they are on vacation. Listen and check (✓) the word
that describes each person.

1. Jill
- ☐ worried
- ☐ excited
- ☐ upset

2. Sean
- ☐ relaxed
- ☐ happy
- ☐ frightened

3. John
- ☐ relaxed
- ☐ pleased
- ☐ worried

4. Rachel
- ☐ happy
- ☐ sick
- ☐ excited

5. Mary
- ☐ upset
- ☐ sick
- ☐ relaxed

6. Margaret
- ☐ bored
- ☐ pleased
- ☐ angry

Task 2

Listen again. Why does each person call? Circle the correct answer.

1. Jill _____ .
- **a.** has some news
- **b.** was in a dangerous situation
- **c.** wants to ask a favor

2. Sean _____ .
- **a.** isn't having a good time
- **b.** has met someone interesting
- **c.** needs money

3. John _____ .
- **a.** lost his wallet
- **b.** lost his ticket
- **c.** will be coming back on time

4. Rachel _____ .
- **a.** has good news
- **b.** needs help
- **c.** to tell her friend about a health problem

5. Mary _____ .
- **a.** lost her glasses
- **b.** was in an accident
- **c.** has good news

6. Margaret _____ .
- **a.** is coming home earlier
- **b.** is taking a different flight
- **c.** doesn't have anything to do

4. Let's Listen 💿

People are describing travel experiences. Is each statement true or false?
Listen and check (✓) the correct answer.

		True	False
1. Cassandra			
	a. She was eating in a Korean restaurant.	☐	☐
	b. She asked the woman to help her.	☐	☐
	c. The woman invited her to join the family at their table.	☐	☐
	d. She hasn't been in touch with the woman since then.	☐	☐
2. Brooke			
	a. She was traveling by train in Italy.	☐	☐
	b. Her wallet was in one of her bags.	☐	☐
	c. Someone stole one of her bags.	☐	☐
	d. The person didn't steal the wallet.	☐	☐
3. Corey			
	a. He had extra clothes with him.	☐	☐
	b. The airline did nothing to help.	☐	☐
	c. His bags arrived four days later.	☐	☐
	d. His bags had important things inside them.	☐	☐
4. Melanie			
	a. She got sick with food poisoning in Australia.	☐	☐
	b. She was only sick for two days.	☐	☐
	c. She knew someone in Sydney.	☐	☐
	d. She went sightseeing for three days.	☐	☐

Task 2

Listen again. Why does each person want to go back again? Write the correct letter.

1. Cassandra ___
2. Brooke ___
3. Corey ___
4. Melanie ___

a. He wants to listen to the traditional music.
b. She wants to see a temple.
c. She wants to see the museums she missed.
d. She wants to scuba dive.

Over to You: Your last vacation

Work in pairs. Answer the questions about your last vacation. Add two questions of your own. Take turns asking and answering the questions with a partner.

1. Where did you go on your last vacation?
   You: _____
   Your partner: _____

2. What did you do while you were there?
   You: _____
   Your partner: _____

3. Did anything unusual happen?
   You: _____
   Your partner: _____

4. Did you lose anything, get lost, or make a new friend?
   You: _____
   Your partner: _____

5. What was the best thing about that vacation?
   You: _____
   Your partner: _____

6. What was the worst thing about that vacation?
   You: _____
   Your partner: _____

7. Other: _____
   You: _____
   Your partner: _____

8. Other: _____
   You: _____
   Your partner: _____